How to
Read the
CATECHISM
OF THE
CATHOLIC
CHURCH
Following
the Liturgical
Year

How to Read the CATECHISM OF THE CATHOLIC CHURCH Following the Liturgical Year

BERNABE DALMAU

LIGUORI
PUBLICATIONS

One Liguori Drive
Liguori, MO 63057-9999
(314) 464-2500

Liguori Publications Edition 1995

This edition published by special arrangement with
Claretian Communications, Inc.
U.P. P.O. Box 4 Diliman, Quezon City 1101, Philippines

ISBN 0-89243-812-6
Library of Congress Card Number: 95-76474

Cover design by Myra Roth
Cover illustration and interior art by Chris Sharp

CONTENTS

INTRODUCTION

On Reading the *Catechism of the Catholic Church*

In some ways, the *Catechism of the Catholic Church* (CCC) is a work that cannot be easily classified. On one hand, there are books that can profitably be read from beginning to end—and that is true of the *Catechism* since it has been conceived as an "organic presentation of the Catholic faith in its entirety" (CCC text paragraph number 18). On the other hand, some volumes are designed primarily for reference and consultation; and certainly the *Catechism* can be used in that way as well.

The *Catechism of the Catholic Church* was conceived as a "*Catechismus maior*"—a major catechism. This was the intention of the fathers of the extraordinary synod of 1985 where the assembled bishops asked for the preparation and publication of a universal catechism. As such, this major work is designed for the bishops and experts in catechesis—and for those who are already well-catechized and who have a good theological foundation.

But a surprising outcome of the publication of the *Catechism of the Catholic Church* in English has been the widespread desire on the part of many ordinary Catholics to read and understand this *Catechism*. But many are intimidated by its length and complexity.

Some potential readers may feel that the *Catechism* may be too heavy and technical. Others may feel incapable of reading the *Catechism* straight through or do not have the time or the inclination to do so. Still others initially may not want to deal with the major organizational factors of the *Catechism*—the significance of larger and smaller sizes of type, the differentiation of the most fundamental truths from those that are complementary, the supporting opinions offered by different ecclesiastical studies as separate from the articles of faith. Finally, some readers may rule out reading the *Catechism* because of its scholarly apparatus, such as footnotes—of which it has many.

Whatever the obstacles, many readers of the *Catechism* probably are not prepared to profit immediately and abundantly from its reading; many may abandon it immediately without even giving it a second chance, and some may not even make an attempt.

That precipitous conclusion would be a pity, since that would mean the loss of the great value of this marvelous work: the presentation of the doctrines of the Catholic Church along with related biblical texts, magisterial or teaching texts, and words from Christian classics.

A Practical Solution

The purpose of this small book, then, is to offer a practical solution to the problems outlined in the previous paragraphs. Our goal is to provide a reader's guide for those who want a simpler introduction to the *Catechism* and who wish to avoid the weightiness and heaviness of some of the material—at least initially. To accomplish this, we have organized selected topics of the *Catechism* around the framework of the liturgical year. Using this approach, the reader can use the *Catechism* devotionally as an instrument to nourish the spirit on a daily basis.

The *Catechism* selections chosen for each day of the liturgical year have been distributed in the same way as has been done with the Sacred Scripture. In making our selections, we have systematically omitted the summary of each *Catechism* topic as well as some pages of secondary importance. As with any selection process, our choices can always be questioned. But we do not doubt that the approach we recommend here is a useful one and can go far to assist the reader in mining the magnificent resources of the *Catechism*.

Distribution of *Catechism* Selections

In slotting the *Catechism* selections in appropriate places in the liturgical year, we have attempted to follow its innate rhythm and dynamic. We have also tried to apply the principle of keeping continuous passages together, along with applying the principle of selecting the most suitable selection for each day. In other words, we have tried to facilitate an equilibrium between suitable text and continuous reading for the sake of sense.

For the great dates of the liturgical year, we have assigned *Catechism* selections that speak most appropriately about the mystery celebrated on that day. And—we have given special attention to the integrity of the liturgical seasons.

Since we consider Easter and Christmas as the great axis of the whole liturgical year, the *Catechism* selections rotate around these two great feasts. Selections relating to the proper texts have been assigned to the Sundays in Advent and to the last nine days. However, *Catechism* selections that refer to the virtues and to happiness have been correlated to the first week of Advent, in consonance with the aura of conversion and hope that is appropriate to this season. The Christmas cycle, after the solemnity of the

Birth of Our Lord, is completed by the *Catechism* texts that refer to the mystery of the Incarnation.

Since the whole sacramental life of the Church emanates from the Resurrection of Christ, *Catechism* topics which treat of baptism are placed after the octave of Easter. However, the topic of confirmation together with the *Catechism* pages dedicated to the Holy Spirit is reserved for the last weeks of Easter, with special reference to Pentecost.

Beginning with the Fourth Sunday of Easter—the Sunday of the Good Shepherd—we present *Catechism* selections pertaining to the sacrament of the priesthood, followed by selections concerning the other sacraments at the service of the community, for example, matrimony. The sacraments of healing—penance and the anointing of the sick—together with the whole *Catechism* theme referred to as sin and grace—are covered during the first weeks of Lent. The explanation of the life of Jesus is allocated to the last weeks of Lent.

Catechism selections have been systematized in the following manner for the weeks of Ordinary Time. The first weeks are dedicated to *Catechism* texts concerning the first articles of the Creed, but we have assigned to the second week of Ordinary Time (the week of prayers for the Unity of Christians) those texts that refer to the mystery of the Church and its unity. As the liturgical year draws closer to the sacraments treated during the Lenten and Easter seasons, we deal with the *Catechism* texts pertaining to the basic notions about the liturgy and the sacramental life.

After Pentecost, at the solemnity of the Holy Trinity, we present the *Catechism* selections about God and revelation. But from the Eleventh Sunday of Ordinary Time, up until the solemnity of the celebration of the Body and Blood of Christ, we deal with *Catechism* texts that concern the Eucharist.

Following that, in connection with the center of sacramental life, we present the entire fourth part of the *Catechism* which is wholly dedicated to Christian prayer. These readings will coincide with the summer months. The final weeks of the liturgical year—those that are after Mission Sunday—are dedicated to those *Catechism* texts dedicated to the last articles of the Creed.

Finally, during the weeks of autumn we can read a selection of topics that concern the third part of the *Catechism* which deals with morals and our life in Christ.

For Whom This Book Is Written

This guide will be useful for all those who really want to read the *Catechism of the Catholic Church*, but who have neither the time nor the courage to read it completely or in an orderly fashion. It can be particularly useful for those who wish to read the *Catechism* in small doses according to a plan that allows meditative reflection on its contents.

This guide may also be helpful for prayer groups and other communities that may need to search for short readings or texts proper for their prayerful consideration on a regular basis. Above all, we feel that the strong correlation of the liturgical year with its seasonal observances and solemnities to the *Catechism* will open a new and fruitful use for this document.

In this way the users of this guide will be able to profit from the work which, according to Pope John Paul II, must serve as the "renewal to which the Holy Spirit is unceasingly calling the Church, the visible body of Christ, in her pilgrimage towards the light of the kingdom."

A Note on the Liturgical Year

On appointed days in the course of the year, the Church celebrates the memory of our redemption by Christ. Throughout the year, the entire mystery of Christ is unfolded. The Church does this in sequence during the various seasons of the liturgical year.

Advent: This season begins four weeks (or slightly less) before Christmas. (The Sunday which falls on or closest to November 30 is its starting point.)

Christmas Season: This season lasts from Christmas until the Baptism of the Lord, the Sunday after Epiphany. (The period from the end of Christmas Season until the beginning of Lent belongs to *Ordinary Time*.)

Lent: The penitential season of Lent lasts forty days, beginning on Ash Wednesday and ending with the Mass of the Lord's Supper on Holy Thursday. The final week is called Holy Week, and the last three days are called the Paschal Triduum.

Easter Season: This season, whose theme is resurrection from sin to life of grace, lasts fifty days, from Easter to Pentecost.

Ordinary Time: This season comprises the thirty-three or thirty-four weeks in the course of the year that celebrate no particular aspect of the mystery of Christ. Instead, the mystery of Christ in all its fullness is celebrated. It includes not only the period between the end of the Christmas Season and the beginning of Lent but also all the Sundays after Pentecost to the last Sunday of the liturgical year (Christ the King).

Proper of Seasons
and
Ordinary Time
of the
Liturgical Year

*Stir us up, O Lord, to make ready
for your only begotten Son.*

ADVENT SEASON

Week of First Sunday of Advent

Day	Catechism Text	Catechism Text Paragraph Number*
Sunday	The Hope of the New Heaven and the New Earth	1042-1047
Monday	The Hope of the New Heaven and the New Earth (continued)	1048-1050
Tuesday	Man: The Image of God	1701-1709
Wednesday	The Beatitudes	1716-1717
Thursday	The Desire for Happiness	1718-1719
Friday	Christian Beatitude	1720-1724
Saturday	The Virtues The Human Virtues	1803 1804

*Each paragraph of the text of the *Catechism* has been given a separate number. These numbers run consecutively from the beginning to the end of the *Catechism*.

Week of Second Sunday of Advent

Day	Catechism Text	Catechism Text Paragraph Number
Sunday	The Eucharist—"Pledge of the Glory to Come"	1402-1405
Monday	The Cardinal Virtues	1805-1809
Tuesday	The Virtues and Grace	1810-1811
Wednesday	Faith	1814-1816
Thursday	Hope	1817-1819
Friday	Hope (continued)	1820-1821
Saturday	Charity	1822-1826

Week of Third Sunday of Advent

Day	Catechism Text	Catechism Text Paragraph Number
Sunday	The Preparations [for the Coming of Christ]	522-524
Monday	Charity (continued)	1827-1829
Tuesday	The Gifts and Fruits of the Holy Spirit	1830-1832
Wednesday	Abraham—"Father of All Who Believe"	145-147
Thursday	Mary—"Blessed Is She Who Believed"	148-149
Friday	Devotion to the Blessed Virgin	971

It is expected that the final days of Advent (celebrated on December 17-24) will begin during the third week. That explains why no Saturday excerpt is listed above.

✛ ✛ ✛ ✛ ✛

Note: The following excerpts are for use between December 17 and December 24. These days will fall partially in the third week of Advent and partially in the fourth week of Advent. These readings should be substituted for those previously given, starting on the calendar date of December 17. If a Sunday follows during this time, use the Sunday excerpt listed below. You may wish to consult a liturgical calendar for the particular year you are using this book.

Final Days of Advent

Day	Catechism Text	Catechism Text Paragraph Number
Sunday	Conceived by the Power of the Holy Spirit	484-486
	…Born of the Virgin Mary	487
December 17	Mary's Predestination	488-489
December 18	God's Spirit and Word in the Time of the Promises	702
	In Creation	703-704
December 19	The Spirit of the Promise	705-706
December 20	In Theophanies and the Law	707-708
	In the Kingdom and the Exile	709-710
December 21	Expectation of the Messiah and His Spirit	711-713
December 22	Expectation of the Messiah and His Spirit (continued)	714-716
December 23	"Rejoice, You Who Are Full of Grace"	721-722
December 24	"Rejoice, You Who Are Full of Grace" (continued)	723-726

Let us be happy, let us celebrate!

Psalm 118

CHRISTMAS SEASON

Christmastime

Day	Catechism Text	Catechism Text Paragraph Number
December 25	The Christmas Mystery	525-526
December 26	The Good News: God Has Sent His Son	422-424
December 27	"To Preach…the Unsearchable Riches of Christ"	425
December 28	[The Name of] Jesus	430-435
December 29	Christ	436-437
December 30	Christ (continued)	438-440
December 31	Why Did the Word Become Flesh?	456-460

✛ ✛ ✛ ✛ ✛

For the Feast of the Holy Family, which usually falls on the Sunday after Christmas, use the following excerpt:

Day	Catechism Text	Catechism Text Paragraph Number
Feast of the Holy Family	The Mysteries of Jesus' Hidden Life	531-534

The Octave of Christmas

Day	Catechism Text	Catechism Text Paragraph Number
January 1 Solemnity of Mary	Mary's Virginal Motherhood in God's Plan	502-507
January 2	True God and True Man	464-467
January 3	True God and True Man (continued)	468-469
January 4	How Is the Son of God Man?	470
January 5	Christ's Soul and His Human Knowledge Christ's Human Will	471-474 475

Celebration of Christ's Coming

Day	Catechism Text	Catechism Text Paragraph Number
Epiphany	The Mysteries of Jesus' Infancy	528
January 7	Christ's Baptism	1223-1225
January 8	Baptism in the Church	1226-1228
January 9	The Mysteries of Christ's Life Christ's Whole Life Is Mystery	512-513 514-515
January 10	Characteristics Common to Jesus' Mysteries	516-518
January 11	Our Communion in the Mysteries of Jesus	519-521
January 12	At the Heart of Catechesis: Christ	426-429
Baptism of the Lord	The Baptism of Jesus	535-537

✛ ✛ ✛ ✛ ✛

Note: All further readings until Ash Wednesday will come from Ordinary Time which starts on page 35. Follow the excerpts given for Ordinary Time until Ash Wednesday.

Return to me with your whole heart,
with fasting and weeping and mourning;
rend your hearts and not your garments,
says the Lord Almighty.

LENTEN SEASON

Week of Ash Wednesday

Day	Catechism Text	Catechism Text Paragraph Number
Ash Wednesday	Interior Penance	1430-1433
Thursday	Why a Sacrament of Reconciliation After Baptism	1425-1426
	The Conversion of the Baptized	1427-1429
Friday	The Sacrament of Penance and Reconciliation	1440
	Only God Forgives Sin	1441-1442
	Reconciliation With the Church	1443-1445
Saturday	The Sacrament of Forgiveness	1446-1449

Week of the First Sunday of Lent

Day	Catechism Text	Catechism Text Paragraph Number
Sunday	Jesus' Temptations	538-540
Monday	The Reality of Sin	386-387
Tuesday	Man's First Sin	397-401
Wednesday	A Hard Battle...	407-409
Thursday	"You Did Not Abandon Him to the Power of Death"	410-412
Friday	Mercy and Sin	1846-1848
Saturday	The Definition of Sin	1849-1851

Week of the Second Sunday of Lent

Day	Catechism Text	Catechism Text Paragraph Number
Sunday	A Foretaste of the Kingdom: the Transfiguration	554-556
Monday	The Different Kinds of Sins	1852-1853
Tuesday	The Gravity of Sin: Mortal and Venial Sin	1854-1860
Wednesday	The Gravity of Sin: Mortal and Venial Sin (continued)	1861-1864
Thursday	The Proliferation of Sin	1865-1869
Friday	"The Kingdom of God Is at Hand"	541-542
Saturday	The Proclamation of the Kingdom of God	543-546

Week of the Third Sunday of Lent

Day	Catechism Text	Catechism Text Paragraph Number
Sunday	The Signs of the Kingdom of God	547-550
Monday	Justification	1987-1991
Tuesday	Justification (continued)	1992-1995
Wednesday	Grace	1996-2000
Thursday	Grace (continued)	2001-2003
Friday	Grace (continued)	2004-2005
Saturday	Christian Holiness	2012-2016

Week of the Fourth Sunday of Lent

Day	Catechism Text	Catechism Text Paragraph Number
Sunday	[Jesus, the] Lord	446-451
Monday	"Jesus Christ Suffered Under Pontius Pilate, Was Crucified, Died, and Was Buried"	571-573
Tuesday	Jesus and Israel	574-576
Wednesday	Jesus and the Law	577-579
Thursday	Jesus and the Law (continued)	580-582
Friday	Jesus and the Temple	583-584
Saturday	Jesus and the Temple (continued)	585-586

Week of the Fifth Sunday of Lent

Day	Catechism Text	Catechism Text Paragraph Number
Sunday	Jesus and Israel's Faith in the One God and Savior	587-589
Monday	Jesus and Israel's Faith in the One God and Savior (continued)	590-591
Tuesday	Divisions Among the Jewish Authorities Concerning Jesus	595-596
Wednesday	Jews Are Not Collectively Responsible for Jesus' Death	597
Thursday	All Sinners Were the Authors of Christ's Passion	598
Friday	"Jesus Handed Over According to the Definite Plan of God" "He Died for Our Sins..."	599-600 601
Saturday	Jesus' Ascent to Jerusalem	557-558

Week of Palm Sunday

Day	Catechism Text	Catechism Text Paragraph Number
Palm Sunday	Jesus' Messianic Entrance Into Jerusalem	559-560
Holy Monday	"For Our Sake God Made Him to Be Sin"	602-603
Holy Tuesday	God Takes the Initiative of Universal Redeeming Love	604-605
Holy Wednesday	Christ's Whole Life Is an Offering to the Father	606-607

Day	Catechism Text	Catechism Text Paragraph Number
Holy Thursday	"The Lamb Who Takes Away the Sins of the World"	**608**
	Jesus Freely Embraced the Father's Redeeming Love	**609**
	At the Last Supper Jesus Anticipated the Free Offering of His Life	**610-611**
Good Friday	The Agony at Gethsemani	**612**
	Christ's Death Is the Unique and Definitive Sacrifice	**613-614**
Holy Saturday	Christ Descended Into Hell	**632-635**

Do you not know that a little yeast
has its effect all through the dough?
Get rid of the old yeast
to make of yourselves fresh dough,
unleavened loves as it were;
Christ our Passover has been sacrificed.

1 Corinthians 5:6

EASTER SEASON

The Week of Easter Sunday

Day	Catechism Text	Catechism Text Paragraph Number
Easter Sunday	Jesus Christ Was Buried	624
	Christ in the Tomb in His Body	625-626
	"You Will Not Let Your Holy One See Corruption"	627
	"Buried with Christ…"	628
Monday	On the Third Day He Rose From the Dead	638
	The Historical and Transcendent Event	639
Tuesday	The Empty Tomb	640
Wednesday	The Appearances of the Risen One	641-644
Thursday	The Condition of Christ's Risen Humanity	645-646
	The Resurrection as Transcendent Event	647
Friday	The Resurrection—A Work of the Holy Trinity	648-650
Saturday	The Meaning and Saving Significance of the Resurrection	651-655

Week of the Sunday Within the Octave of Easter

Day	Catechism Text	Catechism Text Paragraph Number
Sunday	The Liturgical Year	1168-1171
Monday	The Sacrament of Baptism What Is This Sacrament Called?	1213 1214-1216
Tuesday	Prefigurations of Baptism in the Old Covenant	1217-1222
Wednesday	Christian Initiation	1229-1233
Thursday	The Mystagogy of the Celebration	1234-1245
Friday	The Baptism of Adults	1247-1249
Saturday	The Baptism of Infants	1250-1252

Week of the Third Sunday of Easter

Day	Catechism Text	Catechism Text Paragraph Number
Sunday	Faith and Baptism	1253-1255
Monday	The Necessity of Baptism	1257-1261
Tuesday	The Grace of Baptism For the Forgiveness of Sins… "A New Creature"	1262 1263-1264 1265-1266
Wednesday	Incorporated Into the Church, the Body of Christ The Sacramental Bond of the Unity of Christians	1267-1270 1271
Thursday	An Indelible Spiritual Mark…	1272-1274
Friday	One Baptism for the Forgiveness of Sins	977-980
Saturday	Virginity for the Sake of the Kingdom	1618-1620

Week of the Fourth Sunday of Easter

Day	Catechism Text	Catechism Text Paragraph Number
Sunday	The Sacrament of Holy Orders Why Is This Sacrament Called "Orders"?	1536 1537-1538
Monday	The Priesthood of the Old Covenant	 1539-1543
Tuesday	The One Priesthood of Christ Two Participations in the One Priesthood of Christ	1544-1545 1546-1547

Wednesday	In the Person of Christ the
	    Head...
	..."In the Name of the
	    Whole Church"
		
		1548-1551
		
		1552-1553

Thursday	The Sacrament of Matrimony Marriage in God's Plan Marriage in the Order of Creation	1601 1602 1603-1605
Friday	Marriage in the Lord	1612-1617
Saturday	The Celebration of Marriage	1621-1624

Week of the Fifth Sunday of Easter

Day	Catechism Text	Catechism Text Paragraph Number
Sunday	Matrimonial Consent	1625-1632
Monday	The Effects of the Sacrament of Matrimony	1638
	The Marriage Bond	1639-1640
	The Grace of the Sacrament of Matrimony	1641-1642
Tuesday	The Goods and Requirements of Conjugal Love	1643
	The Unity and Indissolubility of Marriage	1644-1645
	The Fidelity of Conjugal Love	1646-1651
Wednesday	The Openness to Fertility	1652-1654
Thursday	The Domestic Church	1655-1658
Friday	The Sacrament of Confirmation	1285
	Confirmation in the Economy of Salvation	1286-1289
Saturday	The Signs and the Rite of Confirmation	1293-1296

Week of the Sixth Sunday of Easter

Day	Catechism Text	Catechism Text Paragraph Number
Sunday	The Celebration of Confirmation	1297-1301
Monday	The Effects of Confirmation	1302-1305
Tuesday	I Believe in the Holy Spirit	683-684
Wednesday	I Believe in the Holy Spirit (continued)	685-686
Thursday	I Believe in the Holy Spirit (continued)	687-688
Friday	The Joint Mission of the Son and the Spirit	689-690
Saturday	"He Ascended into Heaven…"	659-661

Week of the Seventh Sunday of Easter

Day	Catechism Text	Catechism Text Paragraph Number
Sunday	"He Ascended into Heaven…" (continued)	662-664
Monday	The Holy Spirit and the Church in the Liturgy	1091-1092
Tuesday	The Holy Spirit Prepares for the Reception of Christ	1093-1098
Wednesday	The Holy Spirit Recalls the Mystery of Christ	1099-1103
Thursday	The Holy Spirit Makes Present the Mystery of Christ	1104-1107
Friday	The Communion of the Holy Spirit	1108-1109
Saturday	"Come, Holy Spirit"	2670-2672
Pentecost Sunday	Pentecost The Holy Spirit—God's Gift	731-732 733-736

Give thanks to the Lord on the harp,
with the ten-stringed lyre chant his praises.
Sing to him a new song;
pluck the strings skillfully,
with shouts of gladness.

ORDINARY TIME

Week of the First Sunday of Ordinary Time

Day	Catechism Text	Catechism Text Paragraph Number
Sunday	The Baptism of Jesus	535-537
Monday	"I Know Whom I Have Believed"	150-152
Tuesday	Faith and Understanding	156-159
Wednesday	The Freedom of Faith The Necessity of Faith Perseverance in Faith	160 161 162
Thursday	Faith—The Beginning of Eternal Life	163-165
Friday	We Believe "Lord, Look Upon the Faith of Your Church" The Language of Faith	166-167 168-169 170-171
Saturday	Only One Faith	172-175

Week of Prayer for Christian Unity

Day	Catechism Text	Catechism Text Paragraph Number
January 18	"The Sacred Mystery of the Church's Unity"	813-814
January 19	"The Sacred Mystery of the Church's Unity" (continued)	815-816
January 20	Wounds to Unity	817-819
January 21	Toward Unity	820-822
January 22	The Church Is Holy	823-826
January 23	The Church Is Holy (continued)	827-829
January 24	To Bear Witness to the Truth	2471-2474

Week of the Second Sunday of Ordinary Time

Day	Catechism Text	Catechism Text Paragraph Number
Sunday	The Creeds	185-197
Monday	I Believe in God the Father "I Believe in One God"	198 200-202
Tuesday	God Reveals His Name The Living God	203-204 205
Wednesday	"A God Merciful and Gracious" God Alone IS	210-211 212-213
Thursday	God, "He Who *is*," Is Truth and Love God Is Truth	214 215-217
Friday	God Is Love	218-221
Saturday	The Almighty "He Does Whatever He Pleases" "You Are Merciful to All, For You Can Do All Things"	268 269 270-271

Week of the Third Sunday of Ordinary Time

Day	Catechism Text	Catechism Text Paragraph Number
Sunday	The Mystery of God's Apparent Powerlessness	272-274
Monday	The Creator	279-281
Tuesday	Catechesis on Creation	282-285
Wednesday	Catechesis on Creation (continued)	286-289
Thursday	Creation—Work of the Holy Trinity	290-292
Friday	"The World Was Created for the Glory of God"	293-294
Saturday	God Creates by Wisdom and Love God Creates "Out of Nothing"	295 296-298

Week of the Fourth Sunday of Ordinary Time

Day	Catechism Text	Catechism Text Paragraph Number
Sunday	The Visible World	337-341
Monday	The Visible World (continued))	342-344
Tuesday	Man "In the Image of God"	355 356-358
Wednesday	"In the Image of God" (continued)	359-361
Thursday	"Body and Soul But Truly One"	362-368
Friday	Equality and Differences Willed by God "Each for the Other"— "A Unity in Two"	369-370 371-373
Saturday	Man in Paradise	374-379

Week of the Fifth Sunday of Ordinary Time

Day	Catechism Text	Catechism Text Paragraph Number
Sunday	Why the Liturgy?	1066-1068
Monday	What Does the Word Liturgy Mean?	1069-1070
Tuesday	Liturgy as Source of Life	1071-1072
	Prayer and Liturgy	1073
	Catechesis and Liturgy	1074-1075
Wednesday	The Father—Source and Goal of the Liturgy	1077-1083
Thursday	Christ Glorified...	1084-1085
	...From the Time of the Church of the Apostles	1086-1087
Friday	...Is Present in the Earthly Liturgy	1088-1089
	...Which Participates in the Liturgy of Heaven	1090
Saturday	The Paschal Mystery in the Church's Sacraments	1113
	The Sacraments of Christ	1114-1116

Week of the Sixth Sunday of Ordinary Time

Day	Catechism Text	Catechism Text Paragraph Number
Sunday	The Sacraments of the Church	1117-1121
Monday	The Sacraments of Faith	1122-1126
Tuesday	The Sacraments of Salvation	1127-1129
Wednesday	The Sacraments of Eternal Life	1130
Thursday	The Celebrants of the Heavenly Liturgy	1137-1139
Friday	The Celebrants of the Sacramental Liturgy	1140-1141
Saturday	The Celebrants of the Sacramental Liturgy (continued)	1142-1144

Week of the Seventh Sunday of Ordinary Time

Day	Catechism Text	Catechism Text Paragraph Number
Sunday	Signs and Symbols	1145-1149
Monday	Signs and Symbols (continued)	1150-1152
Tuesday	Words and Actions	1153-1155
Wednesday	Singing and Music	1156-1158
Thursday	Holy Images	1159-1162
Friday	Liturgical Seasons	1163-1165
Saturday	The Lord's Day	1166-1167

Week of the Eighth Sunday of Ordinary Time

Day	Catechism Text	Catechism Text Paragraph Number
Sunday	The Sanctoral in the Liturgical Year	1172-1173
Monday	The Liturgy of the Hours	1174-1178
Tuesday	Liturgical Traditions and the Catholicity of the Church	1200-1203
Wednesday	Liturgy and Culture	1204-1206
Thursday	The Anointing of the Sick Illness in Human Life The Sick Person Before God	1499 1500-1501 1502
Friday	Christ the Physician	1503-1505
Saturday	"Heal the Sick…"	1506-1510

Week of the Ninth Sunday of Ordinary Time

Day	Catechism Text	Catechism Text Paragraph Number
Sunday	The Sacrament of the Sick	1511-1513
Monday	The Desire for God	27-30
Tuesday	Ways of Coming to Know God	31-35
Wednesday	The Knowledge of God According to the Church	36-38
Thursday	How Can We Speak About God?	39-43
Friday	God Reveals His "Plan of Loving Goodness"	51-53
Saturday	In the Beginning God Makes Himself Known The Covenant With Noah	54-55 56-58

Week of the Tenth Sunday of Ordinary Time

Day	Catechism Text	Catechism Text Paragraph Number
Sunday	God Chooses Abraham God Forms His People Israel	59-61 62-64
Monday	God Has Said Everything in His Word There Will Be No Further Revelation	65 66-67
Tuesday	"In the Name of the Father and of the Son of the Holy Spirit"	232-237
Wednesday	The Father Revealed by the Son	238-242
Thursday	The Father and the Son Revealed by the Spirit	243-248
Friday	The Formation of the Trinitarian Dogma	249-252
Saturday	The Dogma of the Holy Trinity	253-256

Week of the Eleventh Sunday of Ordinary Time

Day	Catechism Text	Catechism Text Paragraph Number
Sunday	What Is This Sacrament Called?	1328-1332
Monday	The Signs of Bread and Wine	1333-1336
Tuesday	"Do This in Memory of Me"	1341-1344
Wednesday	The Mass of All Ages	1345-1347
Thursday	The Movement of the Celebration	1348-1351
Friday	The Movement of the Celebration (continued)	1352-1355
Saturday	Thanksgiving and Praise to the Father	1359-1361

Week of the Twelfth Sunday of Ordinary Time

Day	Catechism Text	Catechism Text Paragraph Number
Sunday	The Sacrificial Memorial of Christ and of His Body, the Church	1362-1367
Monday	The Sacrificial Memorial of Christ and of His Body, the Church (continued)	1368-1369
Tuesday	The Sacrificial Memorial of Christ and of His Body, the Church	1370-1372
Wednesday	The Presence of Christ by the Power of His Word and the Holy Spirit	1373-1375
Thursday	The Presence of Christ by the Power of His Word and the Holy Spirit (continued)	1376-1379
Friday	The Presence of Christ by the Power of His Word and the Holy Spirit (continued)	1380-1381
Saturday	The Paschal Banquet	1382-1383

Week of the Thirteenth Sunday of Ordinary Time

Day	Catechism Text	Catechism Text Paragraph Number
Sunday	"Take This and Eat It, All of You": Communion	1384-1390
Monday	The Fruits of Holy Communion	1391-1395
Tuesday	The Fruits of Holy Communion (continued)	1396-1398
Wednesday	Prayer in the Christian Life Prayer as God's Gift	2558 2559-2561
Thursday	Prayer as Covenant	2562-2564
Friday	The Universal Call to Prayer In the Old Testament	2566-2567 2568
Saturday	God's Promise and the Prayer of Faith	2570-2573

Week of the Fourteenth Sunday of Ordinary Time

Day	Catechism Text	Catechism Text Paragraph Number
Sunday	Moses and the Prayer of the Mediator	2574-2577
Monday	David and the Prayer of the King	2578-2580
Tuesday	Elijah, the Prophets and the Conversion of the Heart	2581-2584
Wednesday	The Psalms, the Prayer of the Assembly	2585-2589
Thursday	In the Fullness of Time Jesus Prays	2598 2599-2602
Friday	Jesus Prays (continued)	2603-2604
Saturday	Jesus Prays (continued)	2605-2606

Week of the Fifteenth Sunday of Ordinary Time

Day	Catechism Text	Catechism Text Paragraph Number
Sunday	Jesus Teaches Us How to Pray	2607-2612
Monday	Jesus Teaches Us How to Pray (continued)	2613-2615
Tuesday	Jesus Hears Our Prayer	2616
Wednesday	In the Age of the Church	2623-2625
Thursday	Blessing and Adoration	2626-2628
Friday	Prayer of Petition	2629-2633
Saturday	Prayer of Intercession	2534-2536

Week of the Sixteenth Sunday of Ordinary Time

Day	Catechism Text	Catechism Text Paragraph Number
Sunday	Prayer of Thanksgiving	2637-2638
Monday	Prayer of Praise	2639-2643
Tuesday	The Tradition of Prayer At the Wellsprings of Prayer The Word of God The Liturgy of the Church	2650-2551 2652 2653-2654 2655
Wednesday	The Theological Virtues "Today"	2656-2658 2659-2660
Thursday	The Way of Prayer Prayer to the Father Prayer to Jesus	2663 2664 2665-2669
Friday	A Cloud of Witnesses	2683-2684
Saturday	Servants of Prayer	2685-2690

Week of the Seventeenth Sunday of Ordinary Time

Day	Catechism Text	Catechism Text Paragraph Number
Sunday	Places Favorable for Prayer	2691
Monday	The Life of Prayer	2697-2699
Tuesday	Vocal Prayer	2700-2704
Wednesday	Meditation	2705-2708
Thursday	Contemplative Prayer	2709-2712
Friday	Contemplative Prayer (continued)	2713-2719
Saturday	The Battle of Prayer Objections to Prayer	2725 2726-2728

Week of the Eighteenth Sunday of Ordinary Time

Day	Catechism Text	Catechism Text Paragraph Number
Sunday	Facing Difficulties in Prayer Facing Temptations in Prayer	2729-2731 2732-2733
Monday	Filial Trust Why Do We Complain of Not Being Heard?	2734 2735-2737
Tuesday	How Is Our Prayer Efficacious?	2738-2741
Wednesday	Persevering in Love	2742-2745
Thursday	The Prayer of the Hour of Jesus	2746-2751
Friday	The Lord's Prayer: "Our Father!"	2759-2760
Saturday	"The Summary of the Whole Gospel" At the Center of the Scriptures	2761 2762-2764

Week of the Nineteenth Sunday of Ordinary Time

Day	Catechism Text	Catechism Text Paragraph Number
Sunday	The Prayer of the Church	2767-2772
Monday	"We Dare to Say" "Father!"	2777-2778 2779-2785
Tuesday	"Our" Father	2786-2793
Wednesday	"Who Art in Heaven"	2794-2796
Thursday	The Seven Petitions	2803-2806
Friday	"Hallowed Be Thy Name"	2807-2815
Saturday	"Thy Kingdom Come"	2816-2821

Week of the Twentieth Sunday of Ordinary Time

Day	Catechism Text	Catechism Text Paragraph Number
Sunday	"Thy Will Be Done..."	2822-2827
Monday	"Give Us This Day..."	2828-2833
Tuesday	"Give Us This Day..." (continued)	2834-2837
Wednesday	"And Forgive Us Our Trespasses..."	2838-2841
Thursday	"As We Forgive Those Who Trespass Against Us"	2842-2845
Friday	"And Lead Us Not Into Temptation"	2846-2849
Saturday	"But Deliver Us From Evil"	2850-2854

Week of the Twenty-First Sunday of Ordinary Time

Day	Catechism Text	Catechism Text Paragraph Number
Sunday	The Final Doxology	2855-2856
Monday	Life in Christ	1691-1698
Tuesday	Man's Freedom Freedom and Responsibility	1730 1731-1738
Wednesday	Human Freedom in the Economy of Salvation	1739-1742
Thursday	The Morality of Human Acts The Sources of Morality Good Acts and Evil Acts	1749 1750-1754 1755-1756
Friday	Moral Conscience The Judgment of Conscience	1776 1777-1782
Saturday	The Formation of Conscience	1783-1785

Week of the Twenty-Second Sunday of Ordinary Time

Day	Catechism Text	Catechism Text Paragraph Number
Sunday	To Choose in Accord With Conscience Erroneous Judgement	1786-1789 1790-1794
Monday	The Human Community The Communal Character of the Human Vocation	1877 1878-1885
Tuesday	Conversion and Society	1886-1889
Wednesday	Authority	1897-1904
Thursday	The Common Good	1905-1912
Friday	Responsibility and Participation	1913-1917
Saturday	Respect for the Human Person	1929-1933

Week of the Twenty-Third Sunday of Ordinary Time

Day	Catechism Text	Catechism Text Paragraph Number
Sunday	Equality and Differences Among Men	1934-1938
Monday	Human Solidarity	1939-1942
Tuesday	God's Salvation: Law and Grace The Moral Law	1949 1950-1953
Wednesday	The New Law or the Law of the Gospel	1965-1974
Thursday	The Ten Commandments	2052-2055
Friday	"You Shall Love the Lord Your God…" "You Shall Worship the Lord Your God…"	2083 2084-2086
Saturday	The Name of the Lord Is Holy	2142-2149

Week of the Twenty-Fourth Sunday of Ordinary Time

Day	Catechism Text	Catechism Text Paragraph Number
Sunday	The Sabbath Day	2168-2173
	The Day of the Resurrection: the New Creation	2174
	Sunday—Fulfillment of the Sabbath	2175-2176
	The Sunday Eucharist	2177-2179
Monday	The Fourth Commandment	2197-2200
Tuesday	The Fifth Commandment	2258
	The Witness of Sacred History	2259-2262
Wednesday	Peace	2302-2306
	Avoiding War	2307-2317
Thursday	"Male and Female He Created Them"	2331-2336
Friday	The Vocation to Chastity	2337
	The Integrity of the Person	2338-2345
	The Integrality of the Gift of Self	2346-2347
	The Various Forms of Chastity	2348-2350
	Offenses Against Chastity	2351-2356
Saturday	The Love of Husband and Wife	2360-2363
	Conjugal Fidelity	2364-2365

Week of the Twenty-Fifth Sunday of Ordinary Time

Day	Catechism Text	Catechism2 Text Paragraph Number
Sunday	The Fecundity of Marriage	2366-2372
Monday	The Gift of a Child	2373-2379
Tuesday	Adultery Divorce	2380-2381 2382-2386
Wednesday	Other Offenses Against the Dignity of Marriage	2387-2391
Thursday	The Seventh Commandment The Universal Destination...	2401 2402-2406
Friday	Respect for Persons and Their Goods Respect for the Goods of Others	2407 2408-2414
Saturday	Respect for the Integrity of Creation	2415-2418

Week of the Twenty-Sixth Sunday of Ordinary Time

Day	Catechism Text	Catechism Text Paragraph Number
Sunday	The Social Doctrine of the Church	2419-2425
Monday	Economic Activity and Social Justice	2426-2432
Tuesday	Economic Activity and Social Justice (continued)	2433-2436
Wednesday	Justice and Solidarity Among Nations	2437-2442
Thursday	Love for the Poor	2443-2449
Friday	The Eighth Commandment Living in the Truth	2464 2465-2470
Saturday	Offenses Against Truth	2475-2487

Week of the Twenty-Seventh Sunday of Ordinary Time

Day	Catechism Text	Catechism Text Paragraph Number
Sunday	Respect for the Truth	2488-2492
Monday	The Use of the Social Communications Media	2493-2499
Tuesday	Truth, Beauty, and Sacred Art	2500-2503
Wednesday	The Ninth Commandment Purification of the Heart	2514-2516 2517-2519
Thursday	The Battle for Purity	2520-2527
Friday	The Tenth Commandment The Disorder of Covetous Desires	2534 2535-2540
Saturday	The Desires of the Spirit	2541-2543

Week of the Twenty-Eighth Sunday of Ordinary Time

Day	Catechism Text	Catechism Text Paragraph Number
Sunday	"I Want to See God"	2548-2550
Monday	"I Believe in the Holy Catholic Church"	748-750
Tuesday	Names and Images of the Church	751-752
Wednesday	Symbols of the Church	753-757
Thursday	The Church's Origin, Foundation, and Mission	758
	A Plan Born in the Father's Heart	759
	The Church—Foreshadowed From the World's Beginning	760
	The Church—Prepared for in the Old Covenant	761-762
Friday	The Church—Instituted by Christ Jesus	763-766
Saturday	The Church—Revealed by the Holy Spirit	767-768

Week of the Twenty-Ninth Sunday of Ordinary Time

Day	Catechism Text	Catechism Text Paragraph Number
Sunday	The Mystery of the Church	770
	The Church—Both Visible and Spiritual	771
Monday	The Church—Mystery of Man's Union With God	772-773
Tuesday	The Universal Sacrament of Salvation	774-776
Wednesday	The Church—People of God	781
Thursday	Characteristics of the People of God	782
	A Priestly, Prophetic, and Royal People	783-786
Friday	The Church Is Communion With Jesus	787-789
	"One Body"	790-791
Saturday	"Christ Is the Head of This Body"	792-795

Week of the Thirtieth Sunday of Ordinary Time

Day	Catechism Text	Catechism Text Paragraph Number
Sunday	The Church Is the Bride of Christ	796
Monday	The Church Is the Temple of the Holy Spirit	797-798
Tuesday	Charisms	799-801
Wednesday	What Does "Catholic" Mean?	830-831
Thursday	Each Particular Church Is "Catholic"	832-835
Friday	Who Belongs to the Catholic Church?	836-838
Saturday	The Church and Non-Christians	839-845

Week of the Thirty-First Sunday of Ordinary Time

Day	Catechism Text	Catechism Text Paragraph Number
Sunday	Mission—A Requirement of the Church's Catholicity	849-851
Monday	Mission—A Requirement of the Church's Catholicity (continued)	852-856
Tuesday	Why the Ecclesial Ministry?	874-879
Wednesday	The Lay Faithful The Vocation of Lay People	897 898-900
Thursday	The Participation of Lay People in Christ's Priestly Office	901-903
Friday	Participation in Christ's Prophetic Office	904-907
Saturday	Participation in Christ's Kingly Office	908-913

Week of the Thirty-Second Sunday of Ordinary Time

Day	Catechism Text	Catechism Text Paragraph Number
Sunday	The Consecrated Life	914
	Evangelical Counsels, Consecrated Life	915-916
	One Great Tree, With Many Branches	917-919
	The Eremitic Life	920-921
	Consecrated Virgins	922-924
Monday	Religious Life	925-927
	Secular Institutes	928-929
	Societies of Apostolic Life	930
	Consecration and Mission: Proclaiming the King Who Is Coming	931-933
Tuesday	The Communion of Saints	946-948
Wednesday	Communion of Spiritual Goods	949-953
Thursday	"I Believe in the Resurrection of the Body"	988-991
Friday	The Progressive Revelation of the Resurrection	992-996
Saturday	How Do the Dead Rise?	997-1001

Week of the Thirty-Third Sunday of Ordinary Time

Day	Catechism Text	Catechism Text Paragraph Number
Sunday	Risen With Christ	1002-1004
Monday	Dying in Christ Jesus Death	1005 1006-1009
Tuesday	"I Believe in Life Everlasting" The Particular Judgment	1020 1021-1022
Wednesday	Heaven	1023-1029
Thursday	The Final Purification, or 　　Purgatory	1030-1032
Friday	Hell	1033-1037
Saturday	The Last Judgment	1038-1041

The Celebration of Christ the King

Day	Catechism Text	Catechism Text Paragraph Number
Christ the King	Christ Already Reigns Through 　　the Church...	668-670
Monday	...Until All Things Are 　　Subjected to Him	671-672
Tuesday	The Glorious Advent of Christ, 　　the Hope of Israel	673-674
Wednesday	The Church's Ultimate Trial	675-677
Thursday	To Judge the Living and 　　the Dead	678-679
Friday	The Church—Perfected in Glory	769
Saturday	"Amen"	1061-1065

SPECIAL SUNDAYS IN ORDINARY TIME

Day	Catechism Text	Catechism Text Paragraph Number
Holy Trinity Sunday	The Divine Works and the Trinitarian Missions	257-260
Sunday of the Body and Blood of Christ	The Sacrament of the Eucharist The Eucharist—Source and Summit of Ecclesial Life	1322-1323 1324-1327
Sacred Heart of Jesus	Christ's True Body The Heart of the Incarnate Word	476-477 478
Jesus Christ High Priest Forever	The Institution of the Eucharist	1337-1340

✣ ✣ ✣ ✣ ✣

Note: These feasts fall on varying Sundays in Ordinary Time, depending on the cycle (A, B, or C) being used for a particular liturgical year. You may wish to read the selections above on those Sundays of observance or use them as optional readings. Consult a current calendar of the liturgical year if you wish to plot out these specific dates ahead of time.

Proper of Saints
(Feasts and Solemnities)

You are the light of the world.
A city set on a mountain cannot be hidden.
Nor do they light a lamp
and then put it under a bushel basket;
it is set on a lampstand,
where it gives light to all the house.

Matthew 5:14-15

PROPER OF SAINTS (FEASTS AND SOLEMNITIES)

Feast/Catechism Text	Catechism Text Paragraph Number
January 25: Conversion of Paul, Apostle The Life of Man—To Know and Love God	1-3
February 2: Presentation of Jesus Mysteries of Jesus' Infancy	527-530
February 14: Saint Cyril, Religious, and Saint Methodius, Bishop The Grace of the Holy Spirit	1585-1589
February 22: Chair of Peter, Apostle "The Keys of the Kingdom"	551-553
March 19: Joseph, Husband of the Virgin Mary Mary's Virginity Mary—"Ever-virgin"	496-498 499-501
March 25: Annunciation of the Lord "Let It Be Done to Me According to Your Word…" Mary's Divine Motherhood	494 495

April 4: Saint Isidore, Bishop and Doctor
The Heritage of Faith Entrusted to the Whole of
the Church — 84
The Magisterium of the Church — 85-87

April 25: Mark, Evangelist
Inspiration and Truth of Sacred Scripture — 105-108

May 3: Saints Philip and James, Apostles
Mission—A Requirement of the Church's
Catholicity — 849-856

May 14: Matthias, Apostle
The Apostolate — 863-865

May 31: Visitation of Mary to Elizabeth
The Prayer of the Virgin Mary — 2617-2619

June 24: Birth of John the Baptist
John, Precursor, Prophet, and Baptist — 717-720

June 29: Peter and Paul, Apostles
The Only Son of God — 441-445

July 3: Thomas, Apostle
Faith Is a Grace — 153
Faith Is a Human Act — 154-155

July 11: Saint Benedict, Abbot
"The Sabbath—the End of the Work..." — 345-348

July 25: Saint James, Apostle
The Bishops—Successors of the Apostles — 861-862

August 6: Transfiguration of the Lord
"The Gospels Report That..." — 444-445

August 10: Saint Lawrence, Deacon, Martyr
The Three Degrees of the Sacrament of
Holy Orders — 1554
The Ordination of Deacons—"In Order
to Serve" — 1569-1571

August 15: Assumption of Mary into Heaven
…Also in Her Assumption   966
…She Is Our Mother in the Order of Grace   967-970

August 24: Saint Bartholomew, Apostle
The Apostles' Mission   858-860

September 8: Birth of the Virgin Mary
Mary—Mother of Christ, Mother of the Church   963
Wholly United With Her Son…   964-965

September 14: Triumph of the Cross
Jesus Consummates His Sacrifice on the Cross   616-617

September 21: Matthew, Apostle
The Holy Spirit, Interpreter of Scripture   109-114

October 7: Our Lady of the Rosary
In Communion With the Holy Mother of God   2673-2679

October 15: Saint Theresa of Avila
Implications of Faith in One God   222-227

October 18: Luke, Evangelist
The New Testament   124-127

October 28: Simon and Jude, Apostles
…From the Time of the Church of the Apostles…   1086-1087

November 1: All Saints
The Communion of the Church of Heaven
and Earth   954-959

November 2: All Souls
The Meaning of Christian Death   1010-1014

November 9: Dedication of Saint John Lateran Basilica
Where Is the Liturgy Celebrated?   1179-1186

Feast/Catechism Text	Catechism Text Paragraph Number
November 30: Andrew, Apostle	
The Apostolic Tradition	75
In the Apostolic Preaching…	76
…Continued in Apostolic Succession	77-79
December 8: Immaculate Conception	
The Immaculate Conception	490-493

More Catechism-related resources from Liguori...

Faith Alive!
A Study Companion to the Catechism
Faithful to the text of the *Catechism of the Catholic Church* with more inclusive language, *Faith Alive* is a complete presentation of *Catholicism*. Written in a lively, up-to-date style and illustrated with youth-oriented photographs and line drawings, *Faith Alive* will appeal to students as the tool they need to get into the workings of their faith. **$9.95**

Beacons of Light
Profiles of Ecclesiastical Writers Cited in the Catechism
Louis Miller, C.SS.R.
Short biographical sketches and excerpts from the writings of the 73 "ecclesiastical writers" cited in the *Catechism of the Catholic Church*. A fabulous guide to the accomplishments of this diverse group. **$4.95**

Handbook for Today's Catholic
Fully indexed to the Catechism of the Catholic Church
A Redemptorist Pastoral Publication,
Foreword by John Cardinal O'Connor
A guide to Catholic basics. Includes applications of post Vatican II Catholicism, integrating the Catholic faith into everyday life, and Scripture selections. **$2.95**

What You Should Know About the Catechism of the Catholic Church
Charlene Altemose, MSC
This booklet is an absolutely indispensable starting point for basic understanding, intelligent reading, and practical use of the new *Catechism of the Catholic Church!* Without getting bogged down in theology or academics, it carefully explains the new *Catechism*. **$1.95**

Also available... *What You Should Know About the Catechism of the Catholic Church* on audio. One cassette. **$9.95**

Order from your local bookstore or write to
Liguori Publications
Box 060, Liguori, MO 63057-9999
(Please add $2 for postage and handling for prepaid orders under $9.99; $3 for orders between $10 and $14.99; $4 for orders over $15.)